THE MAN WHO KNEW EVERYTHING

THE STRANGE LIFE OF ATHANASIUS KIRCHER

Marilee Peters

Illustrations by
Roxanna Bikadoroff

annick press
toronto + berkeley

ROME, 1655

The carriage rumbled through the maze of narrow, cobblestoned streets. As it passed by, people pointed and chattered. Queen Christina of Sweden, one of the most brilliant and fascinating women in all of Europe, had just arrived in Rome, and the whole city was clamoring to meet her. But the queen had refused all the invitations to glittering parties. Instead, she wanted to go to a museum.

Not just any museum, mind you—the Kircherian Museum, a collection of the most exotic, unusual, and awe-inducing objects the world had to offer.

Finally, the queen's carriage stopped before a long, pale-pink marble building, and her coachman opened the heavy, gilded carriage door. A man in dark priest's robes stood by the building's massive carved entrance. But this was no ordinary priest. This was the most famous scientist in all of Europe.

"Athanasius Kircher," Queen Christina exclaimed as she raced up the steps toward him. "I've been dying to meet you."

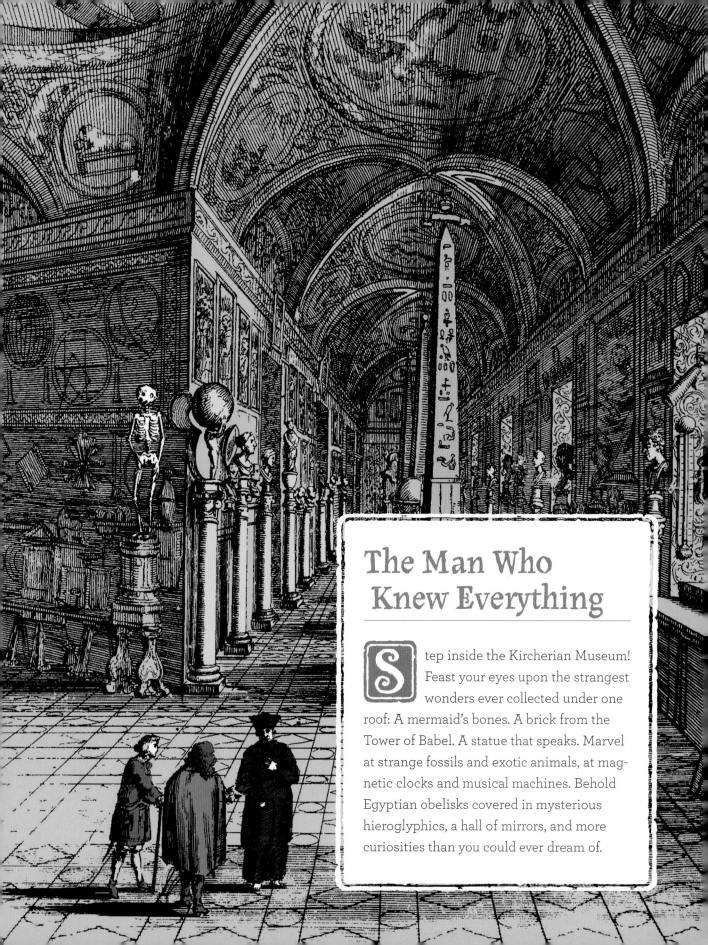

The Man Who Knew Everything

Step inside the Kircherian Museum! Feast your eyes upon the strangest wonders ever collected under one roof: A mermaid's bones. A brick from the Tower of Babel. A statue that speaks. Marvel at strange fossils and exotic animals, at magnetic clocks and musical machines. Behold Egyptian obelisks covered in mysterious hieroglyphics, a hall of mirrors, and more curiosities than you could ever dream of.

How did the Kircherian Museum come to hold all these bizarre and fantastical objects? And who was its mysterious owner—the man Queen Christina had turned down all Rome's wealthy and powerful to meet?

Athanasius Kircher was more than a scientist. He was a star. No single description could contain him. He was an inventor, an author, an adventurer. He published books on music, math, travel, and medicine. He built microscopes and machines. He spoke dozens of languages, and could break secret codes. He claimed to know what lay under the earth, why the sky was blue, and how to tell time using sunflowers and magnets. He had even descended inside an active volcano—and lived to tell the tale! People called him "The Man Who Knew Everything."

Kircher was a curious man, living in a time when there were many more questions about the world than there were answers. And he believed that by asking the right questions, he could understand all the mysteries of the universe.

Did he always get it right? Not even close! His translations of Egyptian hieroglyphics were nonsense. His speaking statue was a fraud. He gave stories and myths the same weight as facts. Kircher was a showman as much as a scientist—closer to P.T. Barnum than to Albert Einstein. So how did he become his era's biggest scientific celebrity, and why are people still fascinated by him today?

The Wonders of the
KIRCHERIAN MUSEUM

If you had visited the Kircherian Museum along with Queen Christina in 1655, here are some of the things you would have seen.

THE VOMITING STATUE

A glass of water "vomited" by a statue of a lobster. For a different flavor, you could try the vomiting eagle or the spitting lady. The statues were funny, but they also demonstrated principles of hydraulics—the movement of liquid.

THE FAN CLUB

Scholars, scientists, and other priests—more than 750 pen pals in all—wrote to Kircher from around the world with news of their discoveries and ideas. He displayed all their letters—a bit like an early version of Facebook.

THE BOX OF MIRRORS

Kircher would place a cat inside to see it spit, snarl, and try to bat away all the "other" cats. Or sometimes he would place a gold coin inside the box and watch people grab at reflections.

A BRICK FROM THE TOWER OF BABEL

This brick supposedly came from the mythical tower described in the Bible, which was said to have reached to the moon. If you asked Kircher, he would explain his calculations proving it wasn't really that high.

THE HIDDEN SHOWER

Kircher loved a joke. On cloudless days, he might predict rain. When his guests scoffed, he'd pull a lever and release water over their heads.

THE LATEST SCIENTIFIC INSTRUMENTS

The museum had telescopes, microscopes, sundials, astrolabes, and globes. Special guests might even be allowed to try them out.

THE SPEAKING ORACLE

Specially built for Queen Christina's visit, this life-sized statue moved its eyes and mouth and answered your questions. (The answers actually came from someone in another room talking down a hollow tube connected to the statue's back).

VENOM-CURING SNAKESTONES

These rocks from India were rumored to be an antidote to snakebites: press the stone against a bite, and it would draw out the poison.

(There's no evidence it really worked.)

BONES FROM A "RACE OF GIANTS"

In Kircher's time, no one knew that mastodons had once roamed Europe. He decided these old bones must have come from ancient supersized humans.

Big Head, Big Ideas

thanasius Kircher was born in 1602, in the German village of Geisa. Like the others in the village, the Kircher house was part stable, part family home. Pigs and chickens rooted and clucked on the main floor. Upstairs, Kircher, his mother and father, and his eight older brothers and sisters slept and ate. Kircher wanted a better life. He dreamed of being a famous author, a scientist, or a scholar, instead of shoveling manure for the rest of his life.

Everyone in the village agreed that the youngest Kircher boy was special. For one thing, he was smart: before he was 12 years old he could read and write in Latin and ancient Greek. Kircher was different in other ways, too. He was insatiably curious about the world around him, asking questions about everything he saw. (His mother claimed it was because he was born with such a big head.) And he was reckless—finding the answers to his questions was more

important to him than staying safe, or even staying alive.

He wondered what kept fish afloat—then fell into a river and nearly drowned trying to find out. He wanted to understand the rhythm of a horse's gallop—and was almost trampled. His mother said he only survived his childhood because his father had insisted on naming him Athanasius, which means "immortal" in Greek. No one in Geisa understood why Kircher risked his life asking questions about the natural world. After all, God had made the world, and that answer was good enough for most people.

By the time Kircher was 16, everyone agreed that he just wasn't suited to village life. His family couldn't afford to send him to university, so he decided to become a Jesuit. The Jesuits are an order of Catholic priests who teach and do missionary work in far-off lands. As a Jesuit, Kircher could study and see the world beyond his little village. It was his ticket to a better life, and his chance to satisfy his burning curiosity about the world.

Then war broke out.

Not just any war, but a long, bitter religious fight between Catholics and a breakaway group called Protestants. In Germany, more than a third of the population died in the conflict, which became known as the Thirty Years' War. In his priest's robes, Kircher was an easy target. For years, he was on the run, dodging Protestant armies. Once, he was captured and nearly hanged by soldiers before he could escape.

Eventually he found his way to Rome.

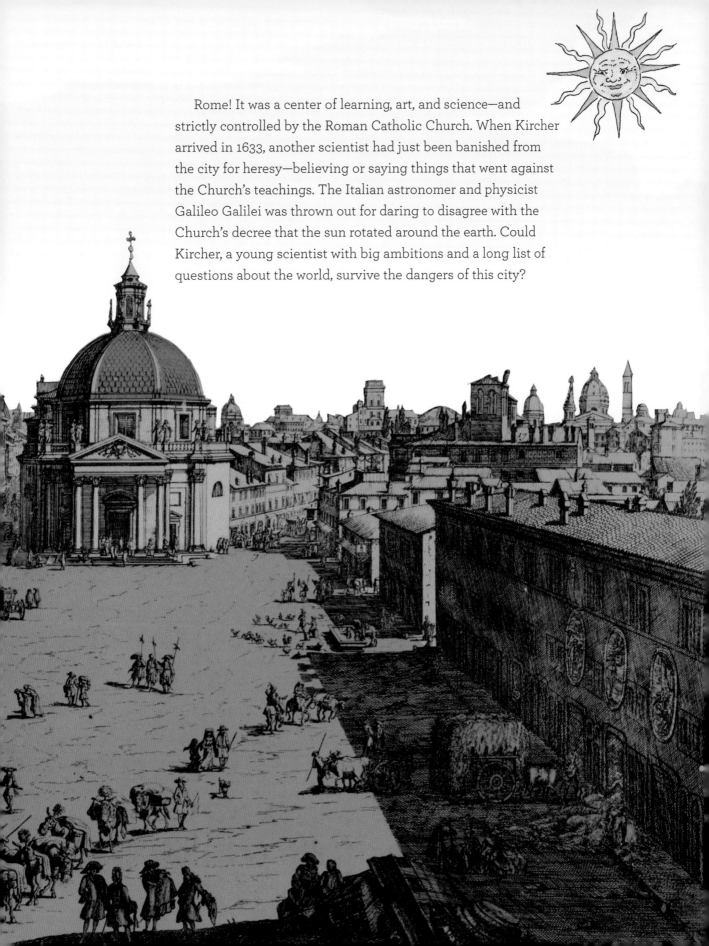

Rome! It was a center of learning, art, and science—and strictly controlled by the Roman Catholic Church. When Kircher arrived in 1633, another scientist had just been banished from the city for heresy—believing or saying things that went against the Church's teachings. The Italian astronomer and physicist Galileo Galilei was thrown out for daring to disagree with the Church's decree that the sun rotated around the earth. Could Kircher, a young scientist with big ambitions and a long list of questions about the world, survive the dangers of this city?

Dangerous Times

Kircher quickly got a job as professor of mathematics at the Roman College, a university for Jesuit priests. Reckless as ever, he didn't let that stop him from investigating anything and everything that interested him. And everything *did* interest him! From math to magnets, from music to medicine, from machines to miracles. Kircher soon became known as the expert with the answers.

THE EARTH'S BIRTHDAY?

During Kircher's lifetime, most Europeans believed that the world was about 6,000 years old. In 1654, a Catholic bishop named James Ussher narrowed down the time of creation to 6 p.m. on October 22, 4004 BCE. Many scientists were skeptical about this strangely precise claim, but at the time there wasn't much evidence to disprove Ussher.

Kircher lived during a time we now call the Scientific Revolution. Scientists and scholars across Europe were beginning to challenge traditional beliefs and use observation and experiments to help them answer questions about the world. But their new ideas weren't accepted overnight.

Just as Protestants had challenged some of the beliefs of the Catholic Church, the new generation of scientists were questioning the "facts" that were the foundation of many people's view of the world. When a Polish astronomer named Nicolaus Copernicus proposed that the earth rotates around the sun—not the other way around—and then Galileo's work proved the theory, it turned the world upside down. As science challenged superstition and myth, people no longer knew what to believe. Were any of their traditional notions correct?

DID I HEAR THAT RIGHT?

Kircher was fascinated with machines that transmitted sound. He built a giant megaphone, and on Saturday afternoons, he hauled it to the hills outside Rome and broadcast orders for everyone to go to church the next day. The first time he tried it, 2,000 people showed up at the local church. His message had been heard five miles away!

Worried that scientific ways of thinking might shake people's faith in God, the Catholic Church tried to stop the spread of dangerous ideas. They started the Inquisition. People with ideas that threatened the Church were arrested, put on trial, or even executed. Galileo wasn't the only scientist to suffer for his heretical ideas: just 50 years earlier, a scientist by the name of Giordano Bruno was burned at the stake.

Kircher knew that if his ideas threatened the Church, he could be banished—or worse. But he wasn't used to playing it safe. Copernicus and Galileo had looked to the skies to find evidence for the earth's place in the cosmos. Kircher looked under his feet instead, and started asking some equally dangerous questions about the world. Were there hidden underground worlds below us? How was the earth constructed? What made the rivers run and the tides flow? How old was the earth? And how could Kircher begin to gather evidence about a part of the world he couldn't even see?

BURNING QUESTIONS

It wasn't just the Catholic Church that persecuted scientists. In 1553, a Protestant doctor named Michael Servetus, who first described the body's circulatory system, was burned at the stake in Geneva, Switzerland.

Volcano Cowboy

or years Kircher wondered about the hidden interior of the earth. Then, quite suddenly, he found an opportunity to look underground—if he were willing to risk his life.

In 1638 he was sailing across the Mediterranean when suddenly clouds of smoke started billowing from a volcanic island called Stromboli. The captain steered the ship toward the safety of the mainland, but before they reached the coast, a moving mountain of water nearly swamped them. The erupting volcano had caused a tsunami—an enormous wave capable of destroying anything in its path.

No sooner had Kircher stepped on shore than the ground began to shake violently, flinging him facedown in the dirt. All around him buildings toppled, bridges crumbled, and people and animals were trapped under falling rubble. Kircher staggered to his feet and wandered the countryside for days, surrounded by ruins and death. It's estimated that 10,000 people died in the Italian earthquake of 1638.

They reached the top just as dawn broke. Against the fading night sky, a billowing plume of smoke rose up, and the shadowy outlines of giant boulders and rocky crags lined the edge of a vast crater.

Kircher had convinced his companion to carry up the biggest wicker basket money could buy, and several long coils of rope. At the volcano's mouth, he announced his plan: to descend into the pit in the basket. His horrified guide tried desperately to change his mind. But Kircher insisted.

While the guide, shaking his head, began unwinding the rope, Kircher gazed into the volcano's crater. His eyes watered, his throat burned from the sulfurous smoke swirling around them, and his heart pounded with excitement and nervousness. What was down there? Would he survive? Swallowing hard, he climbed into the fragile basket. Hand over hand, his guide lowered him slowly into the volcano.

The basket jerked and bashed against the blackened, rocky sides of the crater. Kircher clutched the tools he'd brought along—a chisel to take rock samples, a device to measure the depth of the crater, and his trusty notebook. As the clouds of sulfur cleared, Kircher could see a boiling red lake of lava below him. Then, with a final jolt, the basket stopped. The rope had run out. The priest hung there, twisting and turning, scribbling notes, and leaning out to examine the crater bottom. He could just make out a tunnel opening in one wall, leading away into the darkness. For a moment, he forgot his fear as he imagined what it would be like to follow the tunnel down into the depths of the mountain ...

By the time the groaning guide had hauled Kircher back to the surface, the priest had seen enough for a lifetime of study. His throat and lungs were seared by the smoke and heat, violent coughs racked his body, and he felt so exhausted he could barely

Kircher described the volcano as being exactly like he had always imagined hell: hot, loud, smoky, and terribly stinky!

make it back to the village. But Kircher was overjoyed. He was certain that his rock samples, measurements, notes, and sketches were the beginnings of his greatest work—a book that would explain earth's deepest, most hidden secrets.

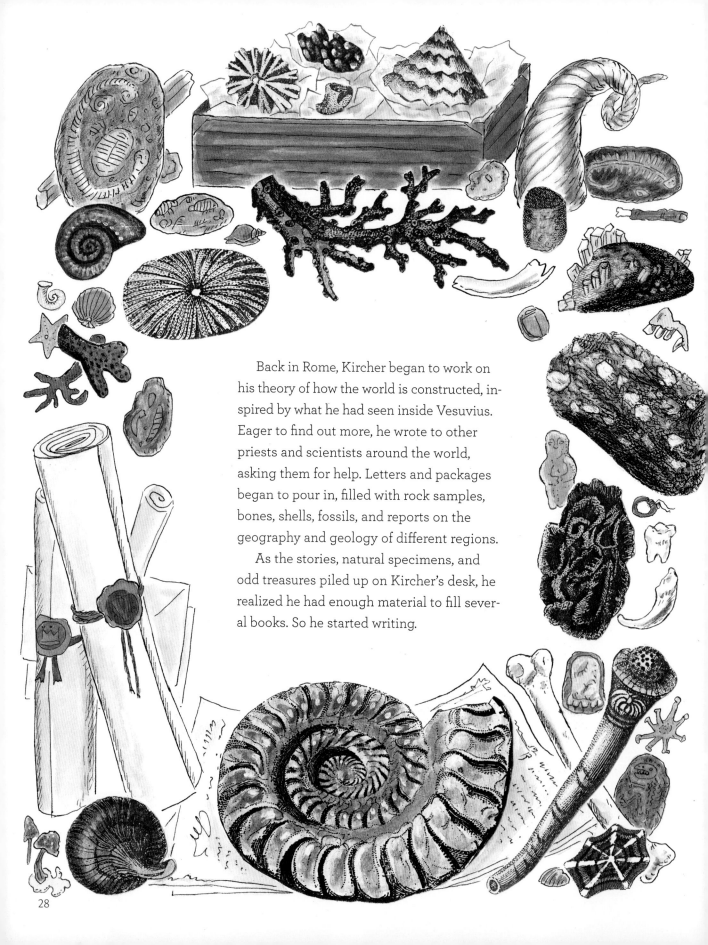

Back in Rome, Kircher began to work on his theory of how the world is constructed, inspired by what he had seen inside Vesuvius. Eager to find out more, he wrote to other priests and scientists around the world, asking them for help. Letters and packages began to pour in, filled with rock samples, bones, shells, fossils, and reports on the geography and geology of different regions.

As the stories, natural specimens, and odd treasures piled up on Kircher's desk, he realized he had enough material to fill several books. So he started writing.

PRODOMO APOLOGETICO
GIOSEFFO di PETRUCCI.

In Amsterdam,
Presso li
VSSONIO WAESBERGI.
Anno 1677.

HUMAN SEARCH ENGINE

Kircher's books covered everything you needed to know about:

- acoustics
- astronomy
- botany
- China
- geography
- geology
- hieroglyphics
- history
- light
- linguistics
- magnetism
- mathematics
- medicine
- music
- secret codes
- songwriting
- science fiction

The Storyteller

Over the next 20 years, Kircher wrote dozens of books about the many topics that interested him. At the same time, he continued to build his grand theory about the world underground. Kircher was one of the first scientists to use his own observations and investigations to understand the natural world. But he also loved a good story. So when someone wrote to tell him about something interesting they'd seen or heard, he'd often include it in his next book simply based on what he'd been told—no matter how unbelievable it might be. The stories made for good reading, but not such great science.

Are bees born from cow manure? Of course not! But Kircher wasn't so sure. Is there a big hole near the South Pole where all the water in the ocean flushes down, like a gigantic drain? Uh, no. But Kircher thought it might explain why the oceans never overflowed. Can you cure a tarantula bite by dancing wildly to loud music? Seems unlikely. It didn't make much sense to Kircher either, but he wrote about it anyway.

Every time he finished a book, he held his breath: Would it pass the censor's review? Would this be the book that brought the Inquisition to his door? Would the Church threaten him with banishment, torture, death? But although the censors sometimes questioned Kircher, they allowed his books to be printed every time.

Meanwhile, exotic oddities from around the world were filling up Kircher's small room at the Roman College. What to do with them all? The answer was simple: show them off.

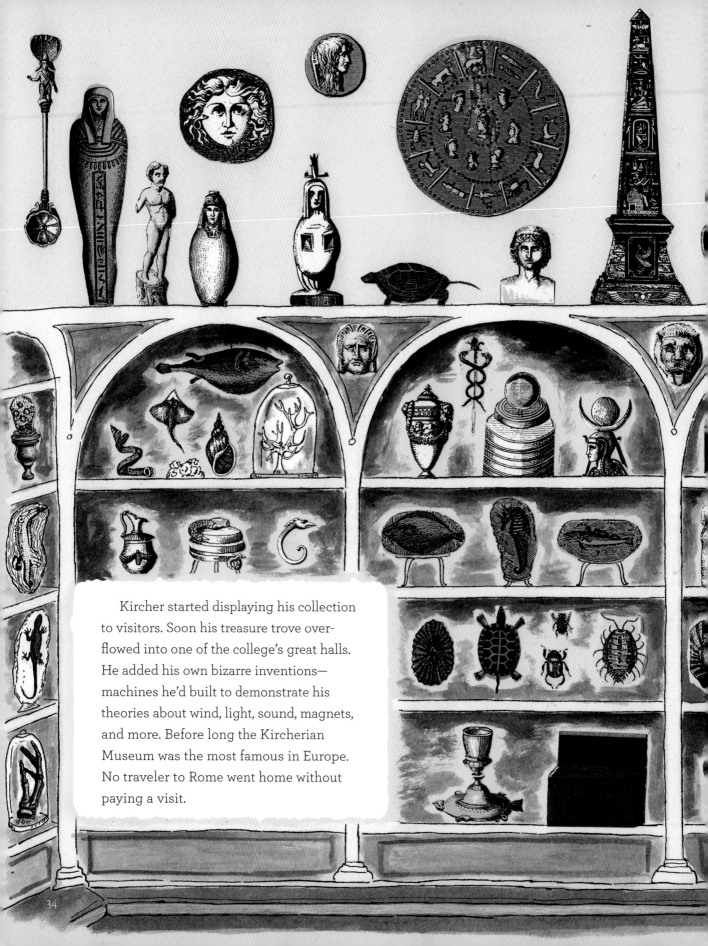

Kircher started displaying his collection to visitors. Soon his treasure trove overflowed into one of the college's great halls. He added his own bizarre inventions—machines he'd built to demonstrate his theories about wind, light, sound, magnets, and more. Before long the Kircherian Museum was the most famous in Europe. No traveler to Rome went home without paying a visit.

CAT MUSIC, ANYONE?

Kircher designed plans for a cat piano, although there's no evidence he actually built it. His idea was to collect a dozen or more cats that meowed in different tones and pitches, and place them in boxes with their tails attached to a piano keyboard. Next, bring in a musician to play some lively music. Every time the musician struck a key, it would yank a different cat's tail. The result? A chorus of yowls, screeches, growls, and howls. Not exactly humane—or musical!

MAGIC LANTERNS

Before movie theaters, photographs, or slide projectors, there was the "magic lantern." It used a candle and a convex mirror to project an image onto a wall. Kircher may not have been the first to invent one, but he described it clearly enough in his books that other people were able to build their own versions, helping to spread and improve the technology. Kircher sometimes took his magic lantern out into the streets at night, projecting images of devils into people's houses to scare them into coming to church!

Going Underground

It took Kircher another 10 years of research, investigation, and thought before he finally published *The Underground World*. It was over 800 pages long, illustrated with dozens of detailed engravings of mountains, underground rivers, fossils, dragons, giants, caves, and maps. Kircher hoped the book would establish his reputation as the greatest scientist of the age.

As one of the first books on geology, *The Underground World* got people thinking about the world in new ways. It became a bestseller, fascinating readers everywhere. But Kircher's love of a good story meant that his science was mixed up with magic and myth. Other scientists and scholars began to question his theories, and distrust his evidence. Sometimes he was right, but more often he was wrong.

PUBLISH OR PERISH?

Kircher wrote all his books by hand, and carefully sketched out his ideas for illustrations. Then he sent the thousands of pages by wagon to his publisher in far-off Amsterdam, hoping the precious bundle didn't get lost or damaged on the way. A small army of artists and engravers worked for months creating elaborate illustrations of his inventions and discoveries. Before it could be published, each book was read by a Church censor to make sure it didn't contain anything heretical. Once it passed, the books were printed and shipped to readers all around the world.

In *The Underground World*, Kircher presented many theories about how the world is constructed.

Theory: Vesuvius's heat is caused by vast underground fires from the center of the earth. The fires force their way through channels up to the surface, emerging as volcanic eruptions. These eruptions keep the planet from overheating.

Truth: Sort of. Volcanoes are ruptures in the earth's crust, through which magma—hot, molten rock—can be forced upwards by pressure.

Theory: Mountains are actually hollow, with channels of fire and water running through them. All European rivers come from a giant underground reservoir located beneath the Alps. The other continents have big reservoirs too—under the Andes, the Himalayas, and the "Mountains of the Moon" in Africa.

Truth: Nope, though underground rivers and lakes do exist.

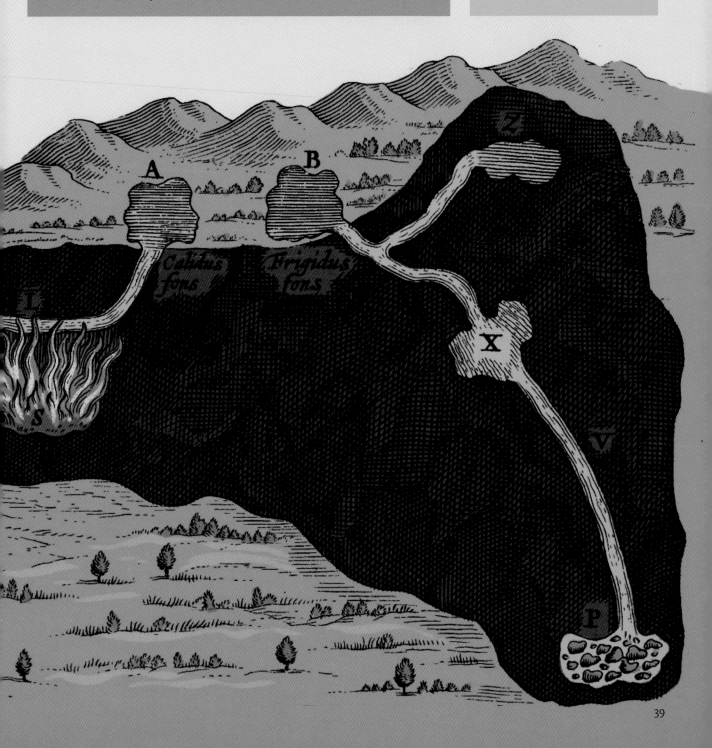

39

Theory: Since rivers eventually empty into the sea, why do the oceans never overflow? Wind forces the sea water down into channels leading under the oceans, eventually filling the mountain reservoirs. The water emerges on the surface in rivers and flows back to the sea.

Truth: Not even close. Oceans don't overflow because water evaporates from the surface and falls back into rivers as rain.

Theory: Because fossilized seashells are sometimes found on mountaintops, the mountains must have been covered by the sea at some point. Earth must make huge movements over vast expanses of time.

Truth: Pretty close. Some mountains were once undersea. And some scientists today think that Kircher's theory sounds like a very early version of plate tectonics—the gradual movement of large pieces of the earth's crust.

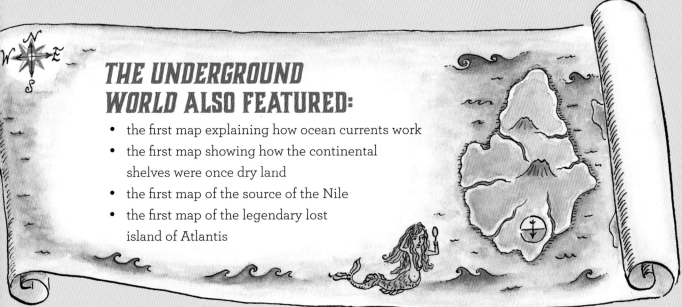

THE UNDERGROUND WORLD ALSO FEATURED:

- the first map explaining how ocean currents work
- the first map showing how the continental shelves were once dry land
- the first map of the source of the Nile
- the first map of the legendary lost island of Atlantis

The Last Renaissance Man

he Kircherian Museum continued to draw crowds of amazed visitors from all over Europe, and Kircher remained at the center of a worldwide network of thinkers who shared their ideas, read each other's books, and tried each other's experiments. Along the way, they created what we call today the scientific method.

But even as Kircher was helping to create science as we know it today, he was being left behind. Younger scientists began to focus their investigations in a single area. They might choose biology, physics, or chemistry—but not all three, and not music, secret codes, or recipes for regrowing plants from burning ashes. Stories, tricks, games, and magic began to be replaced with careful experiments and rational explanations. Kircher's radical methods and his varied interests fell out of fashion.

Quietly, after Athanasius Kircher's death in 1680, at the age of 78, the wonderful objects in the Kircherian Museum were packed away. His books gathered dust in forgotten corners of libraries. And slowly, as people learned more about many things, the world forgot about the wild man of science, the man who had tried to know everything.

Then, in 1988, two young people in Los Angeles, California, opened a museum. Not just any museum, mind you, but a museum devoted to the unusual, the unique, and the exotic. They called it the Museum of Jurassic Technology, and for

their one of their first exhibits they decided to build some of the machines that Athanasius Kircher had written about. They liked the way that Kircher mixed science and magic—and others began to agree. People started to see him as a daredevil scientific pioneer. They began to appreciate his unique blend of information and imagination, good science and old legends, trivia and fact. On Kircher's 400th birthday, a group of his fans gathered for a special debate: "Was Kircher the coolest guy ever, or what?" Since then there have been Kircher clubs, Kircher books, websites, and even a Kircher opera!

Was Kircher a con man, a showman, or a scientist? Maybe all three. What made him successful in his time also ensured he was forgotten for a while, as science became more rational and more specialized. He made huge advancements in scientific knowledge—like germ theory, plate tectonics, and decoding hieroglyphics—but he had more misses than hits. What we remember most today is his risk-taking, his curiosity, and his insatiable need to keep asking questions.

Just after Kircher died, one of his biggest fans realized that there just wasn't a good word to describe Kircher's special contributions to science. So she made one up: to "kircherize" is to make connections between things that seem unrelated. Like volcanoes and rivers, magnets and music, stones and snakebites ... or like a world full of fascinating questions and one man who wanted to know all the answers.

Kircher's
HITS AND MISSES

X MISS!

PREVENT PLAGUE WITH TOAD JEWELRY

In 1656, an epidemic of plague attacked Rome, killing thousands. City leaders begged Kircher to find a cure. He tested all the latest treatments—having your blood drawn, breathing the smoke of burning chemicals, drinking syrup made with powdered snakes—and none of them worked. His tips? To avoid the plague, leave town. If you couldn't, he recommended wearing a dead toad around your neck. Because a toad's skin was blotchy, like a plague victim's, Kircher reasoned the disease would be attracted to it, and not to the wearer.

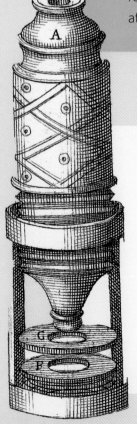

GERM THEORY

Kircher studied blood samples from plague victims under a microscope he'd built himself—one of the earliest in existence. He was startled to see that their blood was full of "worms." His discovery led him to declare that plague was caused by a living organism infecting people's blood. Although he saw microorganisms, Kircher couldn't have actually seen the bacteria that causes plague: he would have needed a powerful compound microscope for that. But he was one of the first scientists to suggest that germs cause disease.

HIT!

GUIDE TO CHINA

Kircher wrote the first guidebook to China, full of fascinating facts about that far-off land. He told of bird's nest soup, Tibetan yaks, and Confucius. He also informed readers that forests in China were filled with rhinoceroses, hippopotamuses, and apes. Of course, Kircher had never actually been to China! Instead, he based his descriptions on letters from Jesuit missionaries, and it seems he mixed in a few notes from Africa by mistake.

HIT AND MISS?

Kircher announced he had cracked the code for translating ancient Egyptian hieroglyphics, 170 years before the Rosetta Stone gave scholars the key. He published translations of the inscriptions on the many Egyptian standing stones, or obelisks, that were found around Rome. Kircher's wild translations were way off base, but he made important discoveries that helped later scholars. He realized that a language called Coptic could provide important clues to deciphering hieroglyphics, and he published the first Coptic dictionary. For his work, some people now call him the Father of Egyptology.

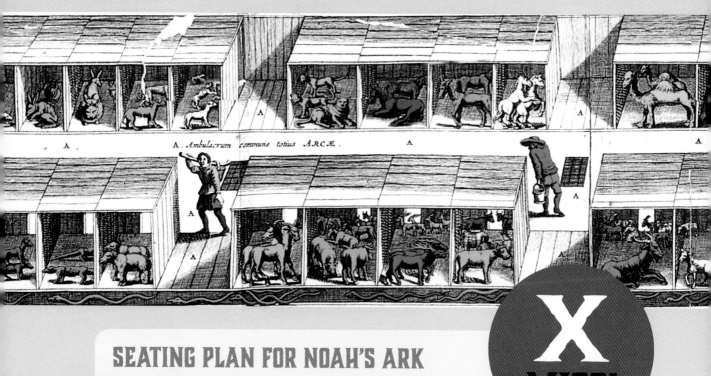

A. *Ambulacrum commune totius* ARCÆ.

SEATING PLAN FOR NOAH'S ARK

Ever wonder how all those animals could have fit in Noah's Ark? Kircher had it all figured out. He published a floor plan for the ark, decided exactly how much room each pair of animals would have needed, and how to arrange them so there weren't any disasters (hint: don't put the mice next to the cats). He even found room for some very unusual passengers: gryphons, mermaids, and unicorns.

X MISS!

X MISS!

SECRET RECIPE FOR SCORPIONS

In *The Underground World*, Kircher wrote that he had generated live scorpions by mixing powdered, dried scorpions with a little water and fresh basil. He also included a recipe for raising frogs from dirt.

MAGNETIC FORCES CONTROL LIFE ON EARTH

Kircher was fascinated by magnets. He thought magnetism was the force behind nearly everything in nature. Why do plant roots grow down? There must be a magnet pulling them toward the center of the earth. Why do flowers reach up for the sun? Because of its magnetic attraction. If the planets are giant magnets, that magnetic push and pull could even explain the rotation of the sun and earth.

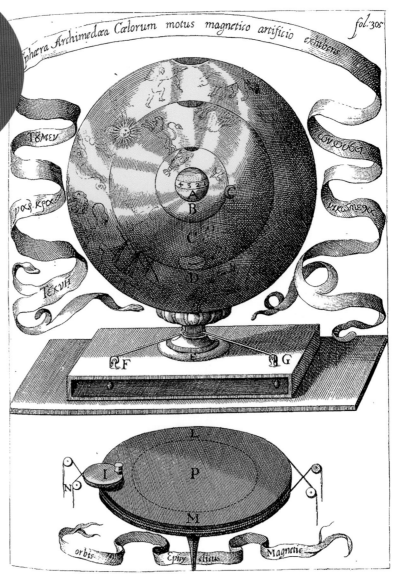

KIRCHER PAVES THE WAY FOR THE THEORY OF GRAVITY

In the 1680s, an English scientist, Sir Isaac Newton, developed the theory of gravity. Like Kircher, Newton focused on magnetism, then realized a different kind of force was at work—gravity. Newton explained that every object, no matter how big or small, exerts a gravitational pull—it tugs other objects toward itself. His theory made sense of everything from the motion of the tides to the orbits of the planets, quickly replacing Kircher's notions about magnetism.

51

Kircher CHRONOLOGY

1618 Thirty Years' War between Protestants and Catholics begins in Germany

1630 Mount Vesuvius erupts for the first time in 500 years

1633 Galileo goes on trial in Rome for suggesting earth revolves around the sun. Convicted of heresy, he is sentenced to house arrest.

1600 **1620** **1630** **1640**

1602 Born May 2 in the town of Geisa, Germany

1618 Enrols in a Jesuit college

1628 Becomes a priest

1631 Publishes his first book, *The Magnetic Art*

1631 Becomes interested in ancient Egypt and starts trying to decipher hieroglyphics

1633 Shipwrecked on the coast of Italy; walks to Rome and begins teaching at the Roman College

1637 Travels to the island of Malta as the companion of a German prince

1638 On his return, experiences a tsunami caused by an earthquake in southern Italy, then numerous aftershocks near Naples; watches the eruption of Mount Etna and Mount Stromboli, then climbs into Mount Vesuvius to investigate whether it appears likely to erupt

1640 Begins exhibiting his inventions and the curiosities he has collected at the Roman College, attracting more and more visitors

1641 Publishes an encyclopedia about magnetism (and much more) using material that other scholars have sent him from around the world

1655 Queen Christina of Sweden abdicates her throne, moves to Rome, and visits the Kircherian Museum

1656 Plague breaks out in Rome, killing thousands

1660 Mount Vesuvius erupts

1650

1660

1988

2002

1651
The museum becomes so large and so popular it is moved into a gallery

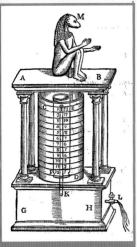

1652
Publishes *The Egyptian Oedipus*, an encyclopedia of his translations of hieroglyphics and his theories about the secrets of the Egyptians

1656
Publishes *Investigation of the Plague*, in which he discusses the source of the deadly illness

Publishes *Ecstatic Journey*, a book about the structure of the universe. Because his ideas contradict the Catholic Church's teachings, Kircher has to be careful: he writes it as fiction. He dedicates the book to Queen Christina.

1660
Publishes *The Great Art of Knowing*, which presents his theories about how someone could actually know everything

1664
After nearly 30 years of work, he publishes *The Underground World*, about his experiences in Vesuvius

1679
Publishes his 30th and last book, *Tower of Babel*

1680
Dies in Rome

1988
The Museum of Jurassic Technology in Los Angeles exhibits reconstructions of some of the machines and inventions Kircher displayed in the Kircherian Museum. A Kircher revival begins.

2002
Kircher's 400th birthday is celebrated with a meeting at New York University to debate "Was Athanasius Kircher the coolest guy ever, or what?"

Kircher's TRAVELS

Follow the numbers to see where Kircher's curiosity took him

4 ... **Cologne, Germany**, but the fighting follows him, so he travels up the Rhine, first to ...

1 Kircher is born in 1602 in **Geisa, Germany**. At 12, he leaves for boarding school in ...

3 ... **Paderborn, Germany**, where he studies until war breaks out. In 1622 he flees to ...

2 ... **Fulda, Germany**. After graduating, he starts college at ...

17 ... **Rome, Italy**, with a lifetime's worth of ideas to write about.

16 ... **Mount Vesuvius, Italy**, where he gets his first look at the secrets of the underground world—inside the volcano! Finally, Kircher heads back to ...

15 ... **Naples, Italy**, where he experiences a massive earthquake. He detours to ...

14 ... **Stromboli, Italy**, where he sees an erupting volcano and is nearly swamped by a tidal wave, so he heads for ...

HISPANIA.

5 ... **Heiligenstadt, Germany**, where soldiers catch him and nearly kill him, and then to ...

6 ... **Koblenz, Germany**, where he builds his first sundial, in 1624. When the fighting moves on, he heads back to ...

7 ... **Heiligenstadt, Germany**, and experiments with making fireworks. It's a blast! He becomes a priest and is offered a job at ...

8 ... **Wurzburg, Germany**, teaching in the University. He first sees hieroglyphics in a library book. But soon, war pushes him onward to ...

9 ... **Lyon, France**, where he's safe from soldiers, but an outbreak of plague forces him to flee to ...

10 ... **Avignon, France**—safe at last! He's happy teaching math and languages at a university. But then he gets a new job offer in Vienna, Austria. He boards a ship in ...

11 ... **Marseille, France**, to cross the Mediterranean on his way to Vienna. The ship is blown off course and lands near ...

12 ... **Rome, Italy**— Kircher's dream come true! He stays put, until in 1637 the pope asks him to take a young prince to ...

13 ... **Malta**. After a year, he's given permission to head back to Rome. On the way back he visits ...

55

FURTHER READING

There are some excellent books for kids on Renaissance scientists:

Adronik, Catherine M. *Copernicus: Founder of Modern Astronomy*. Berkeley Heights, NJ: Enslow, 2002.

Eamer, Claire. *Before the World Was Ready: Stories of Daring Genius in Science*. Toronto, ON: Annick Press, 2013.

Hakim, Joy. *The Story of Science: Newton at the Center*. New York, NY: Smithsonian Books, 2005.

Krull, Kathleen. *Lives of the Scientists: Experiments, Explosions (and What the Neighbors Thought)*. Boston, MA: Harcourt Children's Books, 2013.

Sis, Peter. *Starry Messenger: Galileo Galilei*. New York, NY: Farrar, Straus and Giroux, 1996.

There are no books for kids about Athanasius Kircher, but adults may enjoy:

Glassie, John. *A Man of Misconceptions: The Life of an Eccentric in an Age of Change*. New York, NY: Riverhead Books, 2012.

SOURCES

Alexander, Meredith. "Meet Mr. Know-it-all." *Stanford Magazine*, September 2001. alumni.stanford.edu/get/page/magazine/article/?article_id=39130.

Boxer, Sarah. "A Postmodernist of the 1600s Is Back in Fashion." *New York Times*, May 25, 2002. nytimes.com/2002/05/25/arts/a-postmodernist-of-the-1600-s-is-back-in-fashion.html?pagewanted=all.

Findlen, Paula. "Kircher's Cosmos: On Athanasius Kircher." *The Nation*, April 3, 2013. thenation.com/article/173649/kirchers-cosmos-athanasius-kircher.

Findlen, Paula. *Athanasius Kircher: The Last Man Who Knew Everything*. New York, NY: Routledge, 2004.

Glassie, John. "Athanasius, Underground." *The Public Domain Review*, November 1, 2012. publicdomainreview.org/2012/11/01/athanasius-underground/.

Godwin, Joscelyn. *Athanasius Kircher: A Renaissance Man and the Quest for Lost Knowledge*. London, UK: Thames and Hudson, 1979.

Godwin, Joscelyn. *Athanasius Kircher's Theatre of the World*. Rochester, VT: Inner Traditions, 2009.

Harrington, Ralph. "Athanasius Kircher's 'Mundus Subterraneous' (1664)." *The Volcanism Blog*, June 13, 2009. volcanism.wordpress.com/2009/06/13/athanasius-kirchers-mundus-subterraneus-1664/.

Kircher, Athanasius. *Mundus Subterraneous*. 1665 edition. Translated by P. Conor Reilly. Rome: Edizioni del Mondo, 1974.

Kircher, Athanasius. *The Vulcanos: Or, Burning and Fire-Vomiting Mountains, Famous in the World, with Their Remarkables. Collected for the Most Part out of Kircher's 'Subterraneous World.'* London, 1669.

The Museum of Jurassic Technology website. "Athanasius Kircher, 1602–1680." mjt.org/exhibits/kircher.html.

Rowland, Ingrid D. *The Ecstatic Journey: Athanasius Kircher in Baroque Rome*. Chicago: University of Chicago Library, 2000.

Rowland, Ingrid D. *From Pompeii: The Afterlife of a Roman Town*. Cambridge, MA: Harvard University Press, 2014.

Stolzenberg, Daniel, ed. *The Great Art of Knowing: The Baroque Encyclopedia of Athanasius Kircher*. Stanford, CA: Stanford University Libraries, 2001.

Westfall, Richard S. "Kircher, Athanasius." In The Galileo Project (website), Rice University, 1995. galileo.rice.edu/Catalog/NewFiles/kircher.html.

INDEX

As a kid, Marilee Peters kept a small but very precious collection of curiosities on display in her room: oddly shaped rocks, shells, petrified wood. So when she came to write about Athanasius Kircher and his remarkable museum, she could understand the thrill of showing off a mermaid's skeleton and a unicorn's horn.

Marilee has a passion for telling the stories of forgotten figures in history and overlooked discoveries in science. She is also the author of *Patient Zero: Solving the Mysteries of Deadly Epidemics*. Marilee lives and writes in Vancouver, British Columbia, where she helps to look after the treasure collections of her two children.

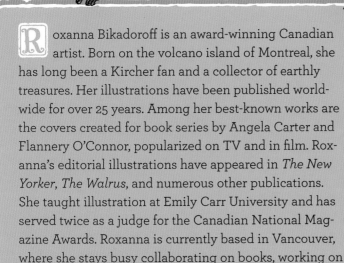

Roxanna Bikadoroff is an award-winning Canadian artist. Born on the volcano island of Montreal, she has long been a Kircher fan and a collector of earthly treasures. Her illustrations have been published worldwide for over 25 years. Among her best-known works are the covers created for book series by Angela Carter and Flannery O'Connor, popularized on TV and in film. Roxanna's editorial illustrations have appeared in *The New Yorker*, *The Walrus*, and numerous other publications. She taught illustration at Emily Carr University and has served twice as a judge for the Canadian National Magazine Awards. Roxanna is currently based in Vancouver, where she stays busy collaborating on books, working on personal projects, and talking to crows.

Colorization of etchings by Bambi Edlund
Cover and interior design by Bambi Edlund
Edited by Barbara Pulling
Proofread by Linda Pruessen

Annick Press Ltd.

We acknowledge the support of the Canada Council for the Arts and the Ontario Arts Council, and the participation of the Government of Canada/ la participation du gouvernement du Canada for our publishing activities.

Funded by the Government of Canada | Financé par le gouvernement du Canada | **Canada**

ONTARIO ARTS COUNCIL
CONSEIL DES ARTS DE L'ONTARIO
an Ontario government agency
un organisme du gouvernement de l'Ontario

Library and Archives Canada Cataloguing in Publication

Peters, Marilee, 1968-, author
The man who knew everything : the strange life of Athanasius Kircher / Marilee Peters ; illustrations by Roxanna Bikadoroff.

Includes bibliographical references and index.
Issued in print and electronic formats.
ISBN 978-1-55451-973-6 (softcover).—ISBN 978-1-55451-974-3 (hardcover).—ISBN 978-1-55451-976-7 (PDF).—ISBN 978-1-55451-975-0 (HTML)

1. Kircher, Athanasius, 1602-1680—Juvenile literature. 2. Scientists—Germany—Biography—Juvenile literature. 3. Intellectuals—Germany—Biography—Juvenile literature. 4. Scholars—Germany—Biography—Juvenile literature. 5. Germany—Biography—Juvenile literature. 6. Volcanology—Juvenile literature. I. Bikadoroff, Roxanna, 1964-, illustrator II. Title.

CT1098.K46P48 2017   j943'.04092   C2017-901410-2
                                        C2017-901411-0

Published in the U.S.A. by Annick Press (U.S.) Ltd.
Distributed in Canada by University of Toronto Press.
Distributed in the U.S.A. by Publishers Group West.

Printed in China

annickpress.com
marileepeters.ca
roxannamundi.ca

Also available in e-book format. Please visit annickpress.com/ebooks.html for more details.

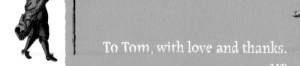

To Tom, with love and thanks.
—MP

To the curious, in the words of Athanasius Kircher,

"The highest mountain, the oldest books, the strangest people, there you will find the stone."
—RB